ALONE,
alone,
alone

MARYANN BELIN BELL

Alone, Alone, Alone

Copyright © 2016 Maryann Belin Bell. All rights reserved. No part of this book may be reproduced or retransmitted in any form or by any means without the written permission of the publisher.

Published by Wheatmark®
1760 East River Road, Suite 145, Tucson, Arizona 85718 USA
www.wheatmark.com

ISBN: 978-1-62787-358-1 (paperback)
ISBN: 978-1-62787-359-8 (ebook)
LCCN: 2015955033

To Anna and Severin Belin,
my beloved parents,
and to my loving family and loyal friends.

Acknowledgments

To all those who have accompanied me through this journey of living life again:

June and Paul Belin, Arminda and A. J. Sandoval, Catherine and David Whitcomb, and Darla and Russell Wolfe.

Thanks also to friends and associates at Busy Bee Printers, The Book Shop in Green Valley, and to my helpful friends at Wheatmark Publishing.

Introduction

Alone, Alone, Alone is my gift to myself and to everyone who has lost his or her lifetime spouse, companion, or loved one to death. Now we are left alone to find our way back to living and enjoying life. We will learn to live in only this moment, looking neither to the past with regret nor to the future with apprehension.

One of my purposes in writing these pages was to help me trust my inner self (my heart), which has led me and will continue to lead me to a profound peace of mind. My goal is to never really worry again and to know that everything I do is taking its intended course. My goal is to be content and to live my best life. I want to be enthusiastic with my new life and learn to accept any and all of my inadequacies. This is my hope for my readers who have and are experiencing the alone syndrome.

As the author of *ALONE, alone, alone*, I have experienced a thorough search of myself and my inner feelings. This has helped me to know and accept myself—to find my personal strength and truths.

It is my hope and commitment that you, the reader, will discover who and what you are and that you will again find and live a life filled with happiness, new experience, and joy.

Life is full of reasons to be happy:
- simple blessings,
- quiet moments
- easy laughter
  and
- sharing these with others.

Everything changes. Nothing is permanent. Approach life with an open mind.

Maryann B. Bell

Contents

I. ALONE, alone, alone 1
The difficult transitional time after the loss of a loved one, when confusion, fear, and loneliness need to be conquered

II. Believe 29
nothing is impossible

III. Challenge 65
your fears and doubts

IV. Determine 89
Your personal quest to live, not exist

V. Enjoy and Energize 125
Every fleeting moment of the mystery of time

I
ALONE, alone, alone

You are reading this book because either you have felt alone or you *are* alone for the majority of your waking hours each day.

Let me clarify, then, that "alone," as this author and millions of others have experienced it, relates to the feeling as well as the actual reality of being alone.

My experience of the alone syndrome began with a lengthy illness of my spouse. It created a new reality of life for me to face and survive each and every day.

We know the reality of life on this earth, with its demands on every waking (and sleeping) hour. Decisions, decisions, and more decisions—all musts for survival.

As earthlings, we also know we are here on borrowed time and that death is inevitable. When will it happen? We don't know, nor do we want to know.

Losing a lifetime spouse or partner is totally devastating, leaving the grieving alone syndrome to adjust to every moment of every day.

The life lived in partnership, through caring, loving, and disagreeing (from time to time), will be totally lost in our new life. Every moment—and I do mean *every* moment—of suffering because of a loved one's death causes hundreds of changes in the remaining person. We must solve this in a forward-moving way to allow ourselves, the remaining partner, to survive being alone (possibly for most of our remaining life on this earth).

For those of us who have lost our partner or spouse, our friends, relatives, neighbors, and associates can be extremely helpful for and during those wonderful everyday-life experiences. Now everything is our challenge to continue to *live* and not just *exist*, to become a totally whole person who must have hope and love deep down inside to build upon and rely on.

Even writing about being alone, which I refer to as "alone syndrome," is difficult, but this continuous search for an inner and outward peace from my heart is an ongoing challenge with strong efforts toward a new way of life.

Each of us must learn to love every moment, looking neither to the past with regret, nor to the future (which is there waiting for us) with apprehension.

We have numerous gifts—faith, love, hope, empathy—deep within us that can hopefully be shared with others each and every day.

Just helping someone to smile instead of crying or becoming too melancholy can help us to feel purposeful and may help that solemn, saddened person to feel a slight lift of feeling good or at least feeling more content.

Feelings are often caused by subliminal messages of pleasantries, patience, and perhaps unreal inward feelings, but we need to face what we *are* as well as what we can be!

The alone syndrome is a very real, profound, moment-by-moment experience. It is almost impossible to describe because it is extremely personal for each of us. As we struggle through it, we can become numb and simply exist from day to day. However, to only exist is not good enough; we must *live*. We have to go beyond our comfort zone and reach out, not especially to others, but in particular to ourselves, looking deep inside our heart, emotionally and psychologically, to find out who we *really* are!

No one can do this for us. It is an unending and continuous task that requires dedication, perseverance, and action. Thinking about this or that, planning, and trying to make improvements will not get us anywhere. We have to *do* it. We have to get it done!

Find some wonderful, fun, happy things to do.

We need to practice the act of *being* and *be* in our choices. If we try something, such as a craft or activity, and find it does not give us a feeling of peace, we must try something else. We must keep trying and not dislike ourselves if we can't say, "This is great! I feel good; I feel happy."

Western society is a couple-oriented world. Couples are everywhere, and rightfully so. But we are *no longer* part of a couple. We are alone—the odd man out. Even though we may have couples who know and love us and are always there for us, the alone syndrome becomes more overwhelming than anyone who hasn't experienced it would realize. We are not left out by them. We feel left out because we are alone—not just lonely, but very deeply alone.

Reaching deeper and deeper into our true selves requires dedication, time, energy, and courage, particularly for those of us who are alone.

We need to practice a simple rather than complicated type of meditation. It is not costly, except for the time we choose to dedicate to it. It helps us to eventually reach our inner selves and have less frustration, personal grief, and feelings of depression and uselessness.

These pages will help in this simple meditation process—to reach our inner selves (sometimes referred to as our soul) and provide quiet, peace, and appreciation for ourselves—a difficult process because we often show more appreciation for others than we show for ourselves!

Do not confuse this feeling with self-centeredness. It is *not* self-centeredness, but instead an avenue or path that needs to be followed as we get to know who we are and where we are going.

As we begin to realize the true uniqueness and inner beauty of who we are, we will know how much we need to start (or continue) thinking from our heart rather than our brain.

Choosing to live from the heart is a personal decision. Only you can choose to live from the heart.

A very dear friend gave me the following poem called "Follow Your Heart":

Follow your heart wherever it takes you,
And be happy
Life is brief and very fragile
and only loaned to us for awhile.
Wake up every morning
with the thought
that something wonderful
is about to happen.

Author: unknown

Our heart has a greater power than anyone realizes. While our brain supports our quest for knowledge to help us make purposeful decisions, our heart is behind absolutely everything we do. Whenever the world (our earthly life) troubles us, we can look to our inner self—to what our heart is speaking—and see how the world with all its realities seems easier to cope with, adding pleasantness and calmness to our lives.

II

Believe

nothing is impossible

Although those of us who have lost loved ones may have many new experiences and a variety of new friends, we are still regularly alone, very often by choice. We may experience a feeling of being paralyzed when we make a commitment to start or accept something new, even if we find it exciting. We are programmed to resist anything that takes us out of our comfort zone.

Inquire, explore, and experience. We need to learn to be open to the helpful suggestions that life is offering—suggestions that could make huge differences in our quality of life.

We have learned that this is our new reality and that every "now" moment is precious because it is life! When we are born, we are issued an invitation to recognize ourselves as a glorious expression of life.

We must commit to a lifelong practice of becoming what we are—a joyful expression of life's invitation—and experience the joy of every moment.

In the present, nothing ever repeats. Past is an illusion. There is no before, just as there is no next. There is only *now*. This moment is new, and you are new; everything is new.

We have the opportunity to live every moment in appreciation of life as it is—which is, by the way, a definition of *joy*.

Life contains everything: the entire range of human emotion, all orientations, and all experiences in various perspectives. The joy of living comes from acceptance of what *is* and from a willingness to respond to life's impulses and move as life moves us.

Living is not a one-time event; it's a lifetime endeavor, and it takes a lifetime of practice. We are in training to realize we are being lived by life. We are learning that awareness is the process of living, the process of life.

If we each get something accomplished a little at a time, we'll always be moving forward. Every day is a good day when you can answer the question "How are you?" with "I'm still above ground." As one of my lifelong friends said to me one day, "Life is to be lived." Life is a gift like no other.

We are on earth to find joy and peacefulness, but it is *not* a given. We must earn it, own it, and realize we are specks of sand in our universe. As unique individuals we are here to contribute not only to our own happiness but also to the joy of everyone, everywhere.

If everyone did his or her small part, what a better life it would be.

Sometimes we need to be terribly brave to follow our inner voice when no one but ourselves can hear or comprehend it. This rocky road from head to heart may not be easy or short, but it may—and eventually will—lead us to our own destiny.

It's like living a creative play—living with mistakes, being given new chances, and making new choices. If we follow our hearts, we'll be doing the things we love doing the most.

We can learn to experience the full spectrum of sensations and emotions available to us in healthy, life-affirming ways.

Being alone after losing a loved one can be (and often is) devastating, but it can also offer that needed time to find out who we really are and to find our new purposes and our new lives. How can we be joyous and happy again?

No one ever said it would be easy. It isn't! We are learning new ways to be content no matter the circumstances. It's a monumental task that might *not* be totally achieved, but it is a primary goal. It is a new and different life for those of us who know the unexpected and often painful newness of our new existence. This life is precious and needs to be *lived*.

My hope and primary goal is that we come to believe and trust in ourselves. We need to live and enjoy the "now moment" as often as possible.

The years slip by all too quickly; there's no time like the present to begin seeking joy in our lives!

If we get ourselves started, we'll find that our lives have taken several new turns, most of which make us feel more comfortable; there are new adventures, new skills, heightened knowledge about various tasks and subjects, new friends, new activities (some creative/artistic), new travels, and new connections.

We need to use our quiet alone time effectively. It is during these solitary "now" moments of meditation that we begin to find an inner peacefulness and joy. Take a little time every day just for yourself, even if it's only fifteen minutes. The joy and happiness we feel in meditation lingers long after we emerge from our sitting. It can stay with us throughout the day, giving us an underlying peace that guides our thoughts, words, and deeds.

We can act from a place of peace and calm. We remain unruffled and undisturbed by life's problems. Living life in such a manner can help heal our mind from its unhealthy and painful thoughts and emotions, allowing us to experience life's joys.

Our inner restlessness reflects a desire and need to understand the mysteries of life. Who are we? What is our purpose?

Without definite answers to these questions, we feel uneasy at times. We want to know the answers but do not know how to find them.

By sitting in meditation for a short period each day, we will experience a calm, loving, peaceful state that can heal our mind, body, and inner self.

We need to learn to fear less and trust more. We need to continuously strive toward being or once more becoming an awakened human.

In every moment, we do make a difference. Every day we impact the world around us. We have choices about the differences we want to make. If we could just spend a little of our time considering the consequences of our choices, more people might also start or restart living lives that are more content and more meaningful.

Each of us can make several small differences daily that, over time, can add up to big differences that we often cannot foresee.

We are unique and can contribute something every moment of our lives, no matter how minimal we may think it is. A kind word or smile can go a long way.

Together, connected with others and working through our very important freedoms of choices, we are powerful and meaningful in the scheme of nature, the connectedness of life.

Because of these connections that act like webs in our lives, we have a responsibility to participate in the real world rather than running and hiding from it.

Reality is not easy to face, especially during stressful and devastating events, but we must move on and be open to life as *it is*.

Losing a loved one changes our entire known world. Insecurity, self-doubt, and self-criticism are just a few aspects of our new "alone" reality, but our lives are *our* message. Every moment that we pledge to believe in ourselves and have an "I can, I will, I do" attitude, we move toward achieving that quest for a happy, purposeful life.

We will find the joy in our lives and pass it on to others. Life is meant to be lived; live it!

III

Challenge

your fears and doubts

Life is like a melody. Each of us is a unique song.

When we tune in to life's wisdom, we feel alive. Each moment is fresh, new, and filled with possibility. There is always something interesting to learn, and we are—or should be—in love with simply finding out. This curiosity—the thrill of adventure, the spirit of inquiry, the joy of discovery—is an orientation that many of us left behind in childhood.

Be open to life as it is *now*. More often than not, we trick ourselves into avoiding the present due to having our attentions consumed by an imaginary future or past. Concentrate on what is actually unfolding here and now.

Being alone puts us in charge. We have to think through problems, make decisions, plan, analyze, synthesize, create, and communicate our thoughts to others.

We face our own emotions of fear, anxiety, tension, confusion, and indecision.

Attachments to an idea of ourselves as constant, permanent entities cause us to resist change, to resist life, to resist what and who we actually are. We are in search of the real truth about ourselves. This is no easy task! We need to *be* in our new life rather than resist it.

A person alone has to transform old habits into newer, more forward-moving habits, toward new adventures and connections in our alone world—a big challenge, a big adjustment.

As human beings, we are often a little fearful and want to stay in our comfort zones. Everything we experienced before our loss created what and who we are now. We have to believe that we can make changes that provide all that life has to offer. Everything in life is connected—the past, the future, the planets, the universe. *Every form of life is connected.*

Our logical mind (our brain) can only show us casual connections, but at the deeper level of our soul, a large web of connections is at work, made apparent by meditation and thoughtful, peaceful moments. We will see these connections, whatever they may be, with our heart (inner being), beyond our own accepted personality. Eventually, through our decision to step out of the box and reach beyond arm's length, new connections will start coming into view, and a new reality will evolve.

Being alone has its merits. We can learn to be more multisensory in connection with our consciousness and inner self. We have to pay attention to how we are finding ourselves very often alone (and not lonely).

We can be at peace and calm with ourselves; it's a very difficult task, but it is very possible when we do new things, evaluate our thoughts, and act on our inner connections and feelings, such as empathy. One of the first symptoms that we have achieved this peace is that we stop worrying! Things don't bother us as much anymore. We learn to become light and full of joy. The second symptom of this peace is that we encounter more and more meaningful coincidences in our new life.

No one wishes the alone syndrome on anyone, but it is a fact of life we must all face.

Millions of others have had to survive the numerous, unending changes to which we have to adjust in order to survive.

The alone syndrome is *real* and begins painfully with feelings of loss and sadness, but each of us who has experienced this life reality must concentrate on accepting the reality of our losses as part of our life experience, even though there are also many instances which are painful and often never ever forgotten.

Once we are aligned with our deeper inner self (our soul) and once we become aware of the hidden order behind our everyday lives, we discover (or rediscover) remarkable patterns and opportunities. Becoming aware of these all-encompassing connections allows even the most insignificant events to be full of meaning.

We all live in a universe, not some small, insignificant, self-chosen space away from the world. We live in a universe of compassion and wisdom. We will learn that these human and personal gifts of our being pervade everything we do. They are always there, but we have to become more aware of these life gifts!

We have to learn to trust in ourselves to conquer our fears! Fear is generally in our imagination. We have to face our fears and recognize that they are not part of our inner self! Only we can redirect these fears into meaningful emotions and events. We are in charge.

As we attempt to accept ourselves and improve ourselves, we begin recreating ourselves and understanding our inner selves. This *inner change* creates *outer change*, and our *inner peace* creates *outer peace*.

The alone syndrome requires inner examination and personal commitment to these concepts, which can be as difficult to *explain* as they are to *accept* and live by.

Live the life you have imagined.

Helen Keller proved to the world, but mostly to herself, that she could conquer more activities than a regular sighted person could achieve. She had more than her share of adversities, but she succeeded in living in the alone world! This is a statement by her about *winning* in an alone syndrome life: "I am only one, but still I am one. I cannot do everything, but still I can do something; I will not refuse to do something I can do."

This is a quote to remember and live by.

Every single day we make a difference. Every single day we impact the world around us, and we have a choice as to what kind of difference we want to make. If we would just spend a little bit of time thinking about the consequences of the choices we make, then we could start living lives that are happier and more meaningful.

Each one of us can make small differences daily that, over time, can add up to big differences that we often cannot foresee!

Every single day we can pledge to ourselves to make a difference that can help us to become happy, loving people who enjoy life.

Each of us *can survive* the alone syndrome.

IV

Determine

your personal quest to live, not exist

Allow plenty of room for what matters most in your life—love, friendship, family, and laughter. Have fun every chance you get.

There is no need for stress and struggle, but we all have challenges to overcome. We *can* do it.

Everything that is meant to be *will be*—with or without our help.

It's easy to get caught up in everyday life—racing the clock, meeting deadlines, shuffling the workload, and becoming so focused on what you *do* that you forget to simply *be*.

A quote often attributed to Mother Teresa is appropriate here:

"Life is an adventure ... dare it."

Be!

Give yourself the freedom to try out new things.

Be open to new ideas, new people, and new adventures.

Find happiness in everything you do.

Open up the windows of your life and let joy shine in.

You are in control of your own thoughts and actions.

Swedish proverb:

> *Fear less, hope more;*
> *Eat less, chew more;*
> *Whine less, breathe more;*
> *Talk less, say more;*
> *Hate less; love more;*
> *And all good things are yours.*

We all need to know that we do not have to be or feel alone; you must give yourself the time to accept the realities of ALONE, alone, alone. As you conquer your own truths, trust yourself.

Find the joy in your life!

You are your own unique masterpiece.

We must discover what we are meant to do, both now and in the long term. We will find our purpose and use our own unique intuitions to allow ourselves to see and feel the things that our hearts and inner beings want us to be. This can lead us to try some new life experiences (e.g., travel, classes, becoming more creative, and stepping out of our self-imposed box).

There's a universe out there waiting for us to tap into its universal connection. We *can* and *will* be on our way to resolving the demanding alone syndrome.

What do we want in life? Think! What does life want of us? Try to be enthusiastic and joyful, not overly stressed! We can and will enjoy the present moment fully; we can enjoy the doing—not just thinking about this or that, but *doing*. We will become more deeply connected with our personal purposes (as we are alone now), and we will find a deeper level of *who* and *what* we are by creating a positive attitude within ourselves.

Earlier in these pages I referred to "we are what we have lived and experienced." But now we are alone, and from here on we are living a *new* life. Every moment is a completely new and different moment because we are the master of ourselves in everything, most, if not all the time.

Love, meaning, and happiness are there to be part of our new life. It's all about seeking and finding and clinging onto joy. The more joy and laughter we seek out and experience, the more joyful we can and will become. Others witness our joy, and often they too become more joyful. A simple smile goes a long way, and it's catchy!

It's very important to have fun. Even in the middle of an activity that requires a lot of discipline, we still need to find this fun—this outer and inner joy.

I decided at age eighty-two to learn how to play the guitar. Even my first lesson was fun, and my not wanting to become a professional guitarist does not affect how happy I feel, deep down inside, and how proud I am that I decided to step out of my personal safety zone and accept the challenges waiting for me. The important point here is that we *can* and *will* find joy in learning something new that will provide us with sound and happy moments.

The alone syndrome (being alone, not lonely) has taught me and is still teaching me not to be troubled by the voices inside me that attempt to discourage me, worry me, and criticize me. I find it best to disregard them and their questions, cutting them off with the words "but what if?"

Learn to accept the new alone syndrome reality by sending loving-kindness (not criticism) and heart and soul energy to yourself. No one ever said it would be easy, but it can be done. "Do it"—these two words are very important and definite but doable words filled with challenges.

The alone syndrome requires us to make changes—all sorts of changes, endless changes. Most of the time we don't want to face the consequences when we make changes, but believing in ourselves and knowing—even reluctantly—that we are committed to making changes can help us try. It will become clear that changes are necessary, and many new possibilities will eventually appear. Making decisions and choices will demand our willingness to take action now, not later.

We need to make lists of the pros and cons of our course of action; our true "self" will tell us what we have to do.

By being prepared as much as possible, we may experience some instant and tangible results.

We have to learn to try different avenues of creativity, including reading, socializing, and enjoying what is around us.

If we don't try, we will not succeed in making changes in our lives. Several instant changes happened to us when we became totally alone, leaving us to do for ourselves everything that someone else used to do for us. This does require an attitude of "I can, I will, I do!" It can be overwhelming and usually is. We need to seek and find a deeper meaning in many everyday situations once we begin to reconstruct our lives. Eventually we will have a renewed enthusiasm for life. We need to continue to seize every opportunity for personal growth, as these will help us feel more at ease with life around us.

We ask ourselves, "What am I learning? What good and joy did this bring into my life?" We need to learn and to see everything that happens in life is a lesson!

We have an obligation in life to connect to others. What does life want from us now, in the present? Are we on the right path to who and what we are or want to become? Alone or not, we are tasked to remake ourselves, as Gandhi's quote implies:

"As human beings, our greatness lies not so much in being able to remake the world as in being able to remake ourselves."

Of course, we have to have knowledge, understanding, acceptance, and intelligence to make decisions and changes, but equally important is having an imagination.

Albert Einstein said,

"Imagination is more important than knowledge, for while knowledge defines everything we know and understand, imagination points to all we might yet discover and create."

We need to rediscover ourselves!

*This final page is reserved for your own photo or painting depicting what **you** enjoy.*

V

Enjoy and Energize

every fleeting moment of the mystery of time

Creativity requires imagination as well as a certain risk! We never really know if our idea is going to materialize the way we conceived! Even so, being creative provides fun. Some efforts and frustrating moments are part of the creative experience, but the results are worth it.

In my efforts to somewhat mitigate the alone syndrome, I have taken several classes and workshops and have created tangible one-of-a-kind items (e.g., bracelets, pendants, beaded necklaces, etc.) to look at, wear, and thoroughly enjoy.

I have enjoyed the planning process and the creative touches added to each individual item. I enjoy the compliments on my creations, but mostly I have enjoyed the fact that I made something unique. I have felt joy and accomplishment with each artistic creation because it was an extension of myself and my willingness to be a *doer*.

Each creative adventure starts with an idea. That idea becomes a reality as we spend time adding special and unique forms and shapes as well as chains (in every length and weight) to finish the creative and artistic endeavors.

Oftentimes, when I wear my glitzy jewelry, people I don't even know will compliment my artistic accomplishments. Moments like these provide me with fond memories and a sense of creative will and fulfillment. Joy and creativity are important parts of my busy and very often alone life!

We do not have to attend classes to be creative because many wonderful books and how-to instructions are available, as are the various craft supplies.

For those of us suffering from the alone syndrome, the toughest task is telling ourselves, "I can, I will, I do." If we plan our day to include something different, no matter how simple it is—calling a friend, addressing a "thinking of you " card, taking a walk or a drive, or going shopping—these happy moments can add variety and joy to our lives every day.

It's also important to treat ourselves. This could be in the way of food, such as candy, an ice cream bar, or a handful of mixed nuts. In our society, we are conditioned to having someone to share our time with food, entertainment, books, paintings, music, volunteer work, and much more. But those of us dealing with the alone syndrome must overcome *being* (and especially *feeling*) alone.

For those who are alone, a tremendous willpower is required to become a strong self in a totally new life. Everything changes instantly; like it or not, it is a shock to our entire mind, body, and feelings. It is a *new reality*. It will always be a tremendous challenge to overcome (however slowly), but that *is* the reality of the alone syndrome—a new method of surviving the stresses and strains and finding peace and joy again, *alone*. It takes effort and time. It takes perseverance and dedication to ourselves—not an egocentric self, but a self we can *accept* as we learn *who we are* and *what* and *who* we will become!

Much of what we will become will be the result of what we do for ourselves (not a selfish self, but a worthy, strong, loving, caring, and sharing self). We need to be kind to ourselves, believe in ourselves, and have faith that we will become stronger and less critical of ourselves.

We need to pat ourselves on our backs, buy ourselves flowers once in a while, and give ourselves a blue ribbon for a top-notch effort! We need to be grateful for our uniqueness and for our willingness to *live* our lives, not just exist.

Gratitude is one of the most powerful things we can do to find peace and tranquility in our new lives!

Whatever happens in our lives, we have to keep faith in a higher order, in the support of something greater than ourselves, always remembering that we are not totally alone; we are actually part of the group of people who are encouraged to learn and to live the alone syndrome lifestyle. We need to remember that even in times of adversity (which one cannot escape entirely), it's a fundamental reality that while we are one body, we are connected to others, as if by a web. Every experience in life moves us in the direction of facing life in the most meaningful way.

Whenever something hurts in life, we usually react in pain, sorrow, exhaustion, and self-criticism. Surviving is a big job for each of us. But we must get rid of these negative feelings now. By prolonging the healing process, we are prolonging the stresses, strains, sadness, and oftentimes guilt. All of these negative responses put the brakes on progressing toward a happy and fulfilled life.

As we strive for self-understanding, fears can escalate if we do not face them honestly. We need to recognize the meaning of each and every fear in order to move forward toward less fearful lives!

The fear-based parts of our personalities are not necessarily enemies. They are there to be conquered, leading us to our inner strengths.

The fear of being alone becomes an extremely powerful fear because we know that eventually we will have to face and conquer it. We must look *within* ourselves to overcome it.

Uniqueness, beauty, love, sadness, joy, creativity, adventure, willingness to adjust and grow are important aspects of life in the NOW moment.

Every day is a new day and it is there for us to enjoy. Every day can have that "something different" from the previous day.

We look for fun, caring, sharing, listening, doing, smiling, hugging, participating, feeling good, being honest (especially with our personal feelings), knowing what and who we are—accepting ourselves, and challenging ourselves to respect and like ourselves more and more as we live each day.

Believe-challenge-determine-enjoy. These are only four focuses of facing the mystery of time. We need to make choices and need to conquer, not submit to being frightful (apprehensive, fearful) about our journey—our new life.

Life's moments move fast. Enjoy these fleeting, precious moments. Help others become part of life's journey, where everyone and everything is connected, unique, and purposeful. By helping others, we are helping ourselves.

As the author of *ALONE, alone, alone*, I want you to remember that there will be a smile and a hug for every tear shed to help you through your sad and troublesome times. These days will soon pass as you find your true and unique self and your purpose through your transition time—where you will find your renewed life of happiness, accomplishment, peace, and joy.

As humans, we want to be happy. It is as fundamental as breathing.

Alone, alone, alone helped me to survive my solitude from the loss of my loved one. As Helen Keller's quote states: "All that we have deeply loved becomes a part of us." We will in some important ways never lose them.

My hope for each reader is that you will find your way to a continuous life of peaceful love and adventure.

Ball on mountain peaks
Bleeds red into passing clouds
Blood moon overhead
           —Russell W. Wolfe

CPSIA information can be obtained
at www.ICGtesting.com
Printed in the USA
BVOW11s1456280416
445781BV00005B/6/P